T0397411

NORSE MYTHOLOGY

THOR

BY HEATHER C. HUDAK

Kids Core
An Imprint of Abdo Publishing
abdobooks.com

abdobooks.com

Published by Abdo Publishing, a division of ABDO, PO Box 398166, Minneapolis, Minnesota 55439. Copyright © 2024 by Abdo Consulting Group, Inc. International copyrights reserved in all countries. No part of this book may be reproduced in any form without written permission from the publisher. Kids Core™ is a trademark and logo of Abdo Publishing.

Printed in the United States of America, North Mankato, Minnesota.
052023
092023

Cover Photo: Shutterstock Images
Interior Photos: Shutterstock Images, 4–5, 11, 14–15, 17 (Sif, Jord), 17 (Frigg, Odin, Thor), 17 (Jarnsaxa), 28 (top), 28 (bottom); Carl Larsson and Gunnar Forssell/Poetic Edda/Wikimedia Commons, 6; Ivy Close Images/Alamy, 9; Pictures From History/Universal Images Group/Getty Images, 10; Gabrielle Photographs/Shutterstock Images, 12; Liliya Butenko/Shutterstock Images, 19, 29 (top); Keith Corrigan/Alamy, 20, 29 (bottom); Marvel Studios/Album/Alamy, 22–23; Chronicle/Alamy, 25; Gabriel Hildebrand/Swedish History Museum, https://mis.historiska.se/mis/sok/fid.asp?fid=107871&g=1, 26

Editor: Katharine Hale
Series Designer: Katharine Hale

Library of Congress Control Number: 2022949116

Publisher's Cataloging-in-Publication Data

Names: Hudak, Heather C., author.
Title: Thor / by Heather C. Hudak
Description: Minneapolis, Minnesota: Abdo Publishing Company, 2024 | Series: Norse mythology | Includes online resources and index.
Identifiers: ISBN 9781098291228 (lib. bdg.) | ISBN 9781098277406 (ebook)
Subjects: LCSH: Mythology, Norse--Juvenile literature. | Thor (Norse deity)--Juvenile literature. | Gods--Juvenile literature. | Divinities--Juvenile literature.
Classification: DDC 293.13--dc23

CONTENTS

CHAPTER 1
Thor and the Giants 4

CHAPTER 2
God of Thunder 14

CHAPTER 3
Worshipped Warrior 22

Legendary Facts 28
Glossary 30
Online Resources 31
Learn More 31
Index 32
About the Author 32

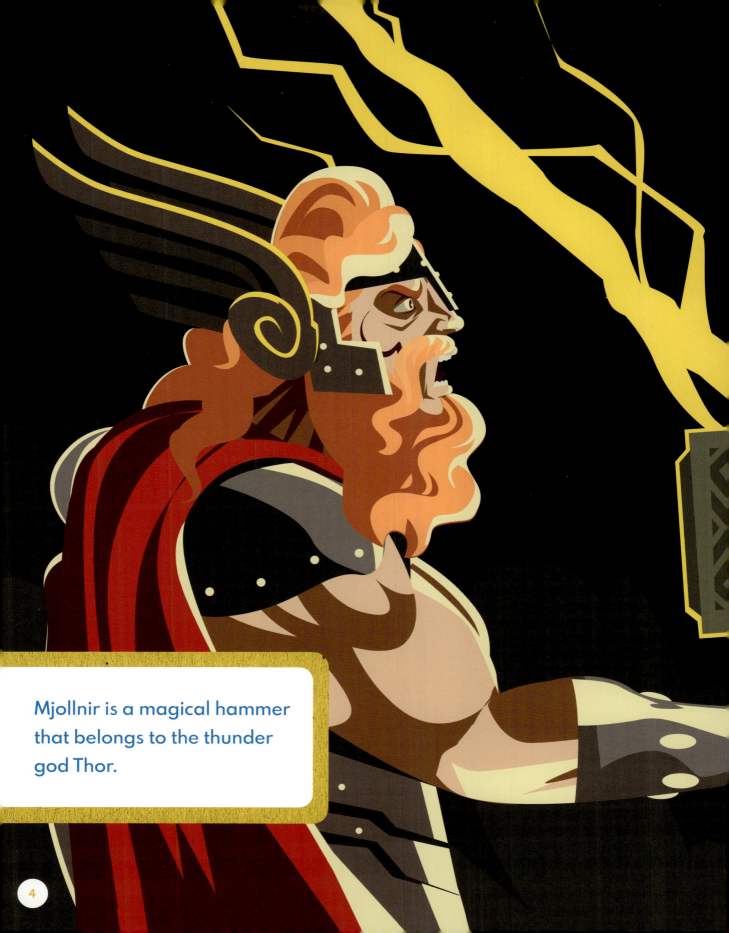

Mjollnir is a magical hammer that belongs to the thunder god Thor.

CHAPTER 1

THOR AND THE GIANTS

Thor was a mighty god. He had a magical hammer called Mjollnir (MEEAWL-neer). Thor used Mjollnir to protect the world and flatten his enemies. He also used it to make lightning. One day, Mjollnir went missing. Thor searched all over.

Thor and Loki dressed as a bride and bridesmaid to get Mjollnir back.

But he could not find his hammer. A giant named Thrym had stolen it. Thrym hid the hammer underground. He would give Mjollnir back only if he could marry the goddess Freya. She refused.

The gods came up with an idea. They would dress Thor up as a bride. He would wear a long dress. A headdress would cover his face. He would pretend to be Freya. Thor did not like this idea. But he really wanted his hammer back. Loki was the Norse **trickster** god. He dressed up as a bridesmaid. The two gods went together to the land of the giants.

Before the wedding, there was a feast. Thor ate an entire ox, eight salmon, and all of the other women's food. Thrym was suspicious. He had never seen a lady eat so much!

But Loki said the bride was so excited about the wedding that she had not eaten in days.

Thrym believed Loki's lies. He laid the hammer in his bride's lap so it could be used to bless the wedding. Thor then removed his disguise. He grabbed his hammer and used it to crush all the giants at the wedding. Thor was glad to have Mjollnir back!

Mjollnir's Origins

Loki bet two dwarfs they could not make the greatest gift anyone had ever seen. If they won, the dwarfs could have Loki's head. But they could not hurt any other part of him. The dwarfs made three gifts. One was Mjollnir. Thor said the dwarfs won. But they could not take Loki's head without hurting his neck. They sewed his mouth shut instead.

Once Thor had his hammer back, he took revenge on the giants.

The Norse named a day of the week after Thor. It was called "Thor's day," which became *Thursday*.

Norse Legends

The Norse people were from **Scandinavia** and northern Germany. The stories from their religion are known today as Norse mythology. Norse myths tell of gods and goddesses who ruled the world. Thor was one of them. There are also stories of elves, dwarfs, giants, and dragons. Some Norse myths date back to the 600s CE or earlier.

The name *Thor* means "thunder."

Thor remains a famous Norse god.

Norse myths were passed down from one generation to the next. The Norse people told these stories **orally**. The myths were not written down until hundreds of years later. There is still much that is unknown about Norse mythology. Most information comes from two books called *The Prose Edda* and *The Poetic Edda*. They were written in the 1200s CE.

Mjollnir is described in *The Prose Edda*:

> Thor would be able to strike whatever came before him with as mighty a blow as he wished, because the hammer would never break. And if he [threw] the hammer, it would never miss its mark, [and it would always] find its way back home to his hand.

Source: Snorri Sturluson. *The Prose Edda*. Translated by Jesse Byock, Penguin Classics, 2005, p. 93.

What's the Big Idea?

Read this quote carefully. What is its main idea? Explain how the main idea is supported by details.

Thor is known for fighting giants.

CHAPTER 2

GOD OF THUNDER

Thor was the god of thunder, the sky, and agriculture. He was a mighty warrior and the strongest of all the Norse gods. He was generally well-mannered, but he had a quick temper. His tantrums could cause thunderstorms.

Family Matters

Thor was tall and muscular. His hair and beard were bright red. Thor's father was Odin. Odin was the leader of the gods. He was a war god worshipped by kings and warriors. Thor was also a war god. But he was worshipped by the common people. Thor's mother was a giantess named Jord, which means "earth."

Thor was married to Sif. She was a beautiful goddess with long, golden hair. Thor and Sif had a daughter named Thrud. Thor was the stepfather of Sif's son, Ull. Thor also had two sons, Modi and Magni. Magni's mother was the giantess Jarnsaxa. Sources are not clear about who Modi's mother is.

Family trees in Norse mythology can be complex.

Symbols of Strength

Thor had three magical items that gave him great power and strength. The first was his hammer. Mjollnir could destroy anything it struck. Thor could throw his hammer anywhere, and it would return to his hand, just

Protecting Gods and Humans

In Norse mythology, the gods lived in Asgard. Earth was called Midgard. Thor watched over both Asgard and Midgard. He used his hammer to protect the gods and keep humans safe from giants, monsters, and other evils. Thor was a man of action. He rarely stopped to think about his next steps.

Thor's goats were named Tanngniost and Tanngrisnir.

like a boomerang. Jarngreipr were iron gloves. They gave Thor the strength to lift his hammer. Megingjard was a magic belt. It doubled Thor's power when he wore it.

Thor rode a **chariot** pulled by two goats. Thor could eat the goats if he was hungry. They would come back to life the next day.

Stories say Thor and Jormungandr will battle at Ragnarok.

Norse people believed thunder was the sound of Thor's chariot wheels. Lightning came when Thor struck giants with his hammer.

End of Time

In Norse mythology, the end of the world is known as Ragnarok. Norse people believed the planet would be destroyed during a battle between good and evil forces. Most of the gods would die. A new world would be created.

Thor's greatest enemy was Jormungandr (YOHR-muhn-gan-der), the Midgard Serpent. Jormungandr was a giant snake, sometimes called a dragon. At Ragnarok, the serpent would rise from the water to fight with Thor. Thor would kill Jormungandr with his hammer. But Thor would die from the snake's **venom**. Modi and Magni would survive Ragnarok. They would use their father's hammer to bring order to the new world.

Further Evidence

Look at the website below. Does it give any new evidence to support Chapter Two?

Thor and the Giants

abdocorelibrary.com/thor

Chris Hemsworth brings Thor to life in the Marvel Cinematic Universe.

CHAPTER **3**

WORSHIPPED WARRIOR

Thor was the most popular Norse god. Just about anyone could pray to Thor if they needed help. Due to Thor's great strength, Norse people often prayed to him to protect them from evil. He was a powerful fighter, and warriors respected him.

Farmers would ask Thor to bring them plentiful crops. Thor ate a great deal of food to keep up his strength. He knew the importance of a good harvest.

Thor was important for more than fighting. People would ask him to bless their weddings or help with marriage problems. They would seek his help in making hard decisions. Thor was

Thor the Superhero

Marvel first introduced Thor in a comic book in 1962. The character is still featured in comics and movies. Marvel's Thor was inspired by Norse mythology. But there are some differences. Marvel's Thor has blond hair, but the Norse god is a redhead. In the comics, Thor and Loki were raised as brothers.

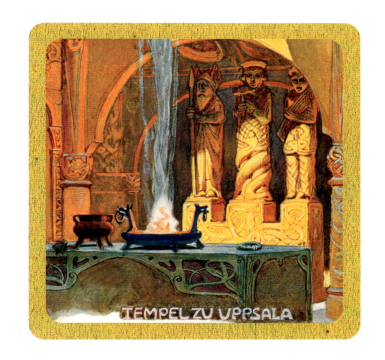

Historians are not sure what the Temple at Uppsala looked like, but they know it existed.

known for his problem-solving skills. He was good at making quick decisions. People would also call on Thor for help if they wanted to have a baby. Much like bringing healthy crops, he could also help bring healthy babies.

Norse religion was mainly practiced at home. But there were some temples honoring Thor. The Temple at Uppsala was located near Sigtuna. This is in modern-day Sweden.

A ring of pendants found in Sweden honors several Norse gods. The Mjollnir pendant represents Thor.

It was built to honor Thor, Odin, and Frey, a **fertility** god. Norse people would make **sacrifices** to the gods at the temple.

Thor in Art

The Norse people created more images of Thor than any other god. People made statues and engravings of Thor. These could be found at temples and shrines across Scandinavia. People wore pendants in the shape of Thor's hammer.

Thor remains famous today. His myths are still popular. But he also has been reimagined for modern media. Versions of Thor appear in video games, books, comics, movies, and more. More than 1,000 years later, Thor continues to influence the world.

Explore Online

Visit the website below. Does it give any new information about Thor that wasn't in Chapter Three?

Thor-ly Mythed

abdocorelibrary.com/thor

LEGENDARY FACTS

Thor is the most famous Norse god.

Mjollnir is Thor's magical hammer.

Thor rides a chariot pulled by goats.

Jormungandr and Thor will fight at Ragnarok.

Glossary

chariot
a small, two-wheeled vehicle that was pulled by animals and was often used for warfare or races

fertility
the ability to create life and support growth

orally
spoken aloud instead of written down

sacrifices
offerings to a god, usually animals or sometimes people

Scandinavia
the countries of Norway, Sweden, and Denmark, and sometimes Iceland and Finland

trickster
a person who plays pranks or tricks on someone else

venom
a toxic material made by animals such as snakes that can cause pain or death

Online Resources

To learn more about Thor, visit our free resource websites below.

Visit **abdocorelibrary.com** or scan this QR code for free Common Core resources for teachers and students, including vetted activities, multimedia, and booklinks, for deeper subject comprehension.

Visit **abdobooklinks.com** or scan this QR code for free additional online weblinks for further learning. These links are routinely monitored and updated to provide the most current information available.

Learn More

Alexander, Heather. *A Child's Introduction to Norse Mythology.* Black Dog & Leventhal, 2018.

Conley, Kate. *Loki.* Abdo, 2024.

Rea, Amy C. *Dragons of Norse Mythology.* Abdo, 2024.

Index

art, 26–27

dwarfs, 8, 10

giants, 7–8, 10, 16, 18, 20
goats, 19

Jarngreipr, 19
Jormungandr, 21

Loki, 7–8, 24,

Marvel, 24
Megingjard, 19
Mjollnir, 5–8, 13, 18–19, 27

Odin, 16, 17, 26

Poetic Edda, The, 12
Prose Edda, The, 12, 13

Ragnarok, 20–21

Scandinavia, 10, 25, 27
Sif, 16, 17

temples, 25–27
thunder, 5, 15, 20

About the Author

Heather C. Hudak has written hundreds of kids' books on all kinds of topics. She loves to travel when she's not writing. Hudak has traveled all over the world, including Germany and Scandinavia. She also enjoys camping with her husband and many pets.